THE KEY TO THE MEN'S CLUB

Opening the doors to women in management

Trudy Coe

Copyright © IM Foundation

First Published 1992

The Institute of Management
Management House
Cottingham Road
Corby
Northants
NN17 1TT

British Library Cataloguing in Publication Data

A CIP catalogue record for this report is available from the British Library

ISBN 0-85946-224-2

CONTENTS

Acknowledgement

This report has been produced with the kind support of BhS plc.

Introduction

Women still account for only three per cent of senior managers and around 9 per cent of the management population as a whole (BIM/Remuneration Economics National Management Salary Survey 1992).

The economic arguments for increasing those proportions should not need rehearsing. Women now make up almost half the work-force and will account for 90 per cent of labour force growth over the next ten years (1).

As the work-force becomes more diverse, the art of management is changing. The traditional command and control culture is giving way to one of involvement and participation. The skills of women managers are ideally suited to the new management environment: research by the Institute of Manpower Studies shows that female employees in general are seen as being more flexible and adaptable and better at team working, managing change, networking and group support (2). If this is true at lower levels of the organisation, should it not apply equally to senior management teams? A board composed entirely of men denies itself the full range of skills needed to tackle increasingly diverse management issues.

If organisations are to be successful in managing diversity and to get the best from all their employees, they can no longer afford to ignore the managerial skills of a large proportion of the work-force. How many companies rule out many of their potential best suppliers or best customers? Yet some are still content to ignore managerial talent in this way.

Many have recognised the scale of this waste and taken action: there are now over 125 signatories to the Opportunity 2000 Campaign who employ over 20 per cent of the work-force. The understanding that all employees do have life beyond the office, and that making it easier for them to manage their lives will increase their effectiveness at work, has gone some way to facilitating a management career for women. Yet there is a danger that focusing on tangible ways of allowing women to combine a family with a traditional management role obscures the real debate. If creche facilities and flexible working are the whole answer, why do so many women still fall behind their male counterparts at the early stages of a management career - even before they have family responsibilities?

The aim of this report was to go beyond the debate about the means to enable women to combine caring and a career; and to explore some of the continuing psychological and attitudinal barriers to the progress of women. Most research to date has focused on identifying the needs of women managers in isolation. This project goes further by exploring both female and male attitudes to women in management.

Detailed questionnaires were sent to all women members of IM and to a parallel sample of male IM members. The women managers provide a unique sample of senior women managers in Britain. They were asked both for details of their personal circumstances and careers in order to establish a profile of successful women managers; and for views on the main barriers they had encountered in those careers. The questionnaire to men sought to establish any differences in personal and career profiles; and then explored men's attitudes to the role of women in management.

The results give the first detailed breakdown of differing attitudes to women in management. Analysis of them sheds much light on why the barriers to the progress of women remain so high. That analysis is used to form a series of practical recommendations for employers and government.

Key Findings

Women IM members are more senior than women managers in general. At most levels of management they are nearly as well represented as their male counterparts. The exception is at the very top: 7 per cent describe themselves as chair/chief executive compared to 15 per cent of men.

- 20 per cent of the women surveyed run their own business - the same proportion as for men. The majority of both men and women entrepreneurs employ fewer than 10 people.

- The women in the sample are much more likely than men to work in a service industry, in education or training or in government. They also tend to be concentrated in support roles: only 1 per cent are in a manufacturing or production function.

- Only 3 per cent of the women work part time and only 1 per cent have a flexible working pattern.

- Women IM members are better qualified than men: 44 per cent have a post-graduate / Masters degree or equivalent qualification against 28 per cent of men.

- The women are several years younger on average than the men. Only 68 per cent are married (92 per cent of men). 12 per cent are divorced or separated (5 per cent of men).

- Fifty two per cent of the women have had a caring responsibility for children or for elderly or disabled relatives against 88 per cent of the men.

- 37 per cent of the women currently have caring responsibilities at present against 70 per cent of men. These differences cannot be entirely attributed to age differences between the two samples - or to differing interpretations of 'caring responsibility'.

- The impact of caring on the women's careers is much greater. 42 per cent of the women who have had a caring responsibility say it has affected their career against only 16 per cent of men.

- Women gave 'difficulty in working long hours' and 'need to work locally' as the main reasons for the adverse effect of caring.

- 54 per cent of the women and 51 per cent of men believed it was possible to combine a career in management and a caring responsibility only at 'considerable personal cost'.

- 29 per cent of the women had taken a break for child care and 10 per cent for training. 39 per cent of those taking a break to care for children had returned at a lower management grade, compared to only 15 per cent of those who took time off for training. Of those taking a break for training, 44 per cent returned at a higher level.

- Only 20 per cent of the women anticipate internal promotion as the next step in their management career, compared to 36 per cent of men.

- Women perceived 'the existence of the men's club network' as the greatest barrier to women in management, followed by prejudice of colleagues.

■ Attitudinal barriers were all perceived as greater obstacles than tangible ones such as lack of child care. Divorced and single women are more likely to rate attitudes as a barrier than their married colleagues.

■ The majority of the women say they have received most support during their career from partner or family - including those who are single. Employers are generally seen as unsupportive of female managers.

■ One third of the women feel they do not receive adequate respect from male superiors. 13 per cent felt that the attitude of their organisation to women managers was 'negative' or 'very negative': only a quarter thought it was very positive.

■ Only 35 per cent of the men 'strongly agree' that women managers bring positive skills to the work-place, against 74 per cent of women. 18 per cent of men - and 12 per cent of women - admit they do or would find it difficult to work for a woman manager.

■ The women were more likely to favour greater government support for child care: 64 per cent of women and 41 per cent of men thought tax relief should be extended to all forms of child care.

■ Few organisations provide help for their women managers or for carers in general. The most common form of help given is special training. Here, provision exceeds need: 37 per cent of the women said their organisations provide it but only 33 per cent believe it should be provided.

■ In every other area, there is a vast gap between provision and expectations. 43 per cent of the women would like help with child care, but only 9 per cent of their organisations provide it; 49 per cent would like assistance for carers but only 6 per cent of their organisations provide it.

Profile of Women Managers

The research

Questionnaires were mailed in May 1992 to all 2,532 women members of the then British Institute of Management (BIM)*. A parallel questionnaire was mailed to a random sample of the same number of male BIM members. Both questionnaires are reproduced at Annex A.

1,457 women returned the questionnaire by 29 June, a response rate of 58%. 797 men replied by the same date, a response rate of 30%. Reply paid envelopes were enclosed with both questionnaires.

Both male and female members were invited to comment - on a non- attributable basis - on individual questions and on the general issues raised by the questionnaires. Several hundred comments were received and it is not possible to reproduce them all in the report. Those that were representative are used to illustrate the research findings.

BIM's 1989 survey

The survey follows an interim survey in 1989 of BIM's women members (3). At that time there were 2,400 women in membership. 800 responded by the deadline, a response rate of 33 per cent.

The aims of the 1989 survey were to record a description of BIM's women members and to establish a detailed file of information about the needs of women managers. It was less comprehensive than the current one, and there are few exact matches between the questions. Where possible, however, comparisons are drawn between the two surveys to highlight any differences between the samples.

The proportion of women in management

Nationally, it is difficult to obtain accurate figures on the proportion of women in management. Estimates vary depending upon the definitions used within organisations, functions or industries. A middle manager in a large organisation is a senior one in a small business.

A 1990 report by NEDO (4) estimated that 27 per cent of managers were women, but only 4 per cent at middle

or senior level, falling to 1 or 2 per cent at chief executive level.

More recent evidence is supplied by the 1992 BIM National Management Salary Survey (5). This covers over 20,000 individuals employed by 340 companies. In the 1992 Survey, 8.6 per cent of the sample were female.

These proportions are reflected among IM's own membership. Overall, 5 per cent of members are female; the proportion rises to 13 per cent for new registrations.

Managerial level

Women IM members are not representative of the female management population as a whole. They appear to be more senior than women managers in general and approximate fairly closely in seniority to their male counterparts. 32 per cent describe themselves as senior managers (35 per cent for men) and 26 per cent as middle management (21 per cent for men). Only 7 per cent are junior managers.

Even within this sample, women are less well represented at the very top. Only 7 per cent describe themselves as chair or chief executive against 15 per

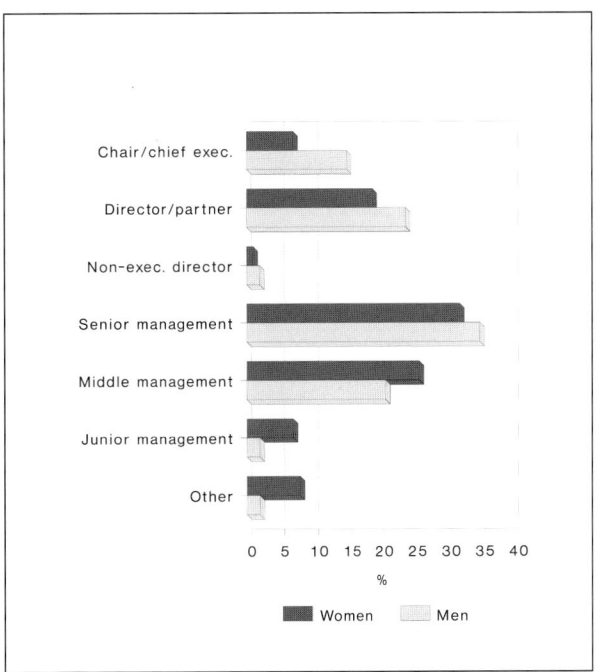

Fig 1 - Managerial level

* BIM and the Institution of Industrial Managers merged with effect from 1 November 1992 to form the new Institute of Management (IM).

5

cent of men; and 19 per cent as directors or partners, against 24 per cent of men.

There is little difference between male and female respondents in relation to managerial level and size of company: 50 per cent of women and 52 per cent of men describe themselves as senior managers in companies with over 1,000 employees.

Cross analysis of these results with responses to later questions shows that there is little correlation between the management level reached by women and their family circumstances. The women with children in this sample are just as likely - or equally unlikely - to reach the top.

It is difficult to determine whether there have been any changes since 1989, given the differences between the two samples and the different way in which this question was phrased in 1989. Then, 49 per cent described themselves as head of department or division, 19 per cent were directors and 12 per cent chief executives. The apparent fall in the number of women at the top is more likely to be a reflection of sampling differences than a significant change in the number of women reaching senior managerial positions.

Age of respondents

Some of the differences in managerial level between male and women IM members can be attributed to age differences between the two samples. Women are on average several years younger than their male counterparts: 17 per cent of women managers are below 35 compared to only 4 per cent of men. The largest number of women are between 35 and 44 (45 per cent) whereas the largest proportion of men are between 45 and 44 (again 45 per cent).

There are some differences between the 1989 and 1992 samples of women managers. In 1989, 24 per cent of women were between 25 and 34, whereas only 16 per cent are now. There has been a corresponding rise in the number of women between 45 and 54: 31 per cent in 1992 against 25 per cent in 1989.

Business ownership

There is a remarkable similarity between the numbers of male and female managers running their own business. 20 per cent of the women respondents run their own company, compared to 19 per cent of men.

The profile of companies run by both men and women entrepreneurs is similar. The majority of women (59 per cent) and men (57 per cent) running their own companies have fewer than 10 employees. 13 per cent

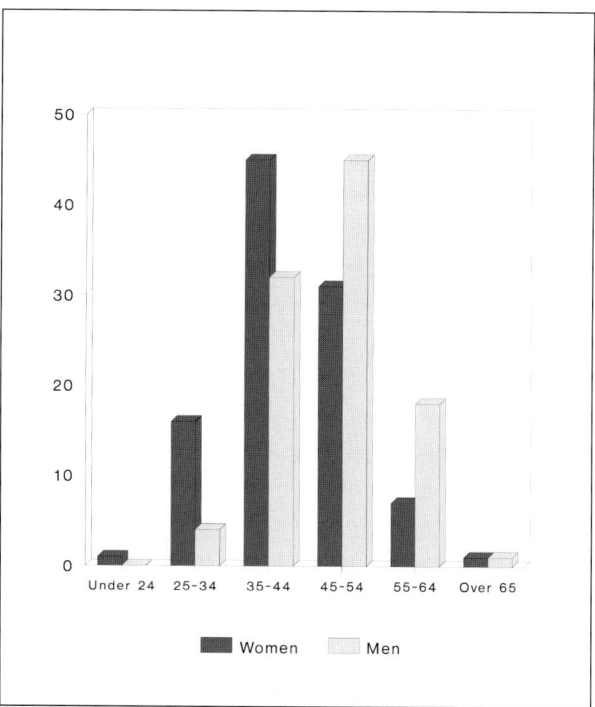

Fig 2 - Women and men age differences

of women and 8 per cent of men employ over 100 employees (these two sub-samples are very small).

Women and men are setting up very similar companies in terms of activity. In each case, roughly a third operate as management consultants. This reflects clearly IM's own membership profile and the survey provides little evidence to support the general view

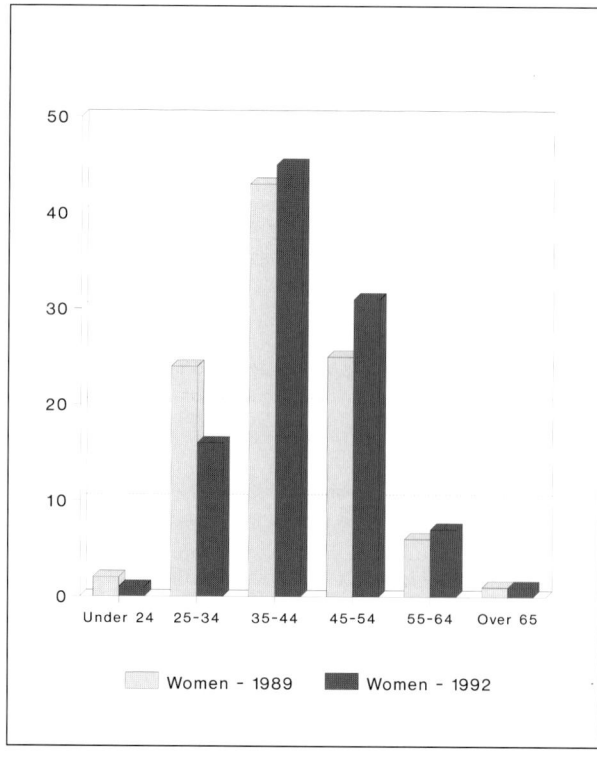

Fig 3 - Age differences women 1989 and 1992

that, where women set up their own business, they tend to do so in the 'soft' or service industries such as catering or retail.

The number of women running their own business increases with age. Of those between 55 and 64, 31 per cent run their own company against 13 per cent of those between 25 and 34. The same trend is apparent in relation to the age of men running their own company.

The proportion of women entrepreneurs has declined slightly since 1989, when it was 24 per cent. The difference is too slight to draw firm conclusions, although it is possible to speculate that women may now be finding it marginally easier to pursue mainstream management careers rather than turning to setting up their own business.

There have been slight changes since 1989 in the age of women entrepreneurs. Fig 5 shows the percentages of each age sample in both years who run their own company. The numbers have fallen in each category except the very youngest (small sample size) and the oldest.

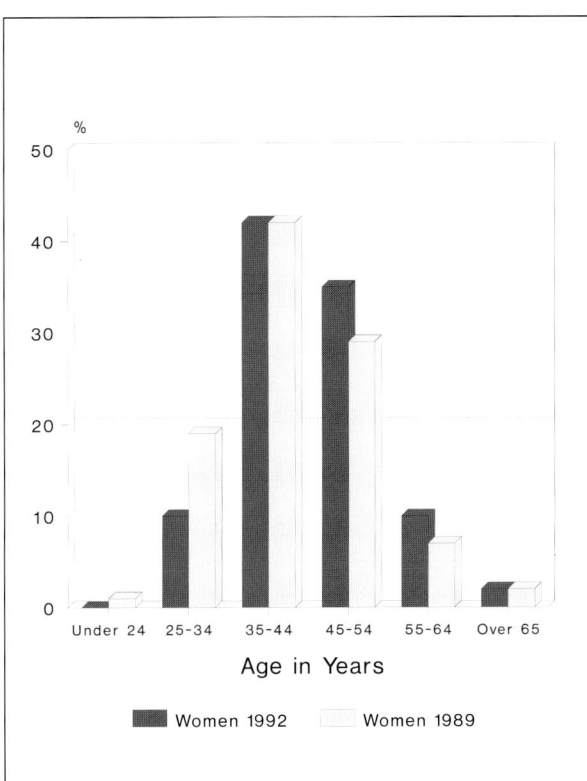

Fig 5 - Age differences for women running their own company 1989 and 1992

women are in an education or training function against 6 per cent of men, while only 1 per cent of women managers work in a production or manufacturing function compared to 6 per cent of men.

The only changes of note since 1989 are an increase from 8 to 13 per cent in women working in a company secretary or administration function, and an increase from 11 to 15 per cent in the numbers working in education.

Management function

	Women %	Men %
General management	21	31
Education/training	15	6
Administration	13	7
Other	12	12
Personnel/HR/IR	8	3
Management consultancy	8	7
Finance/accounting	6	8
Marketing/sales	6	8
Management services	3	3
Computing/IT	3	3
Development/strategic affairs	2	2
Purchasing/contracting	1	3
Production/manufacturing	1	6
Corporate affairs/PR	1	0

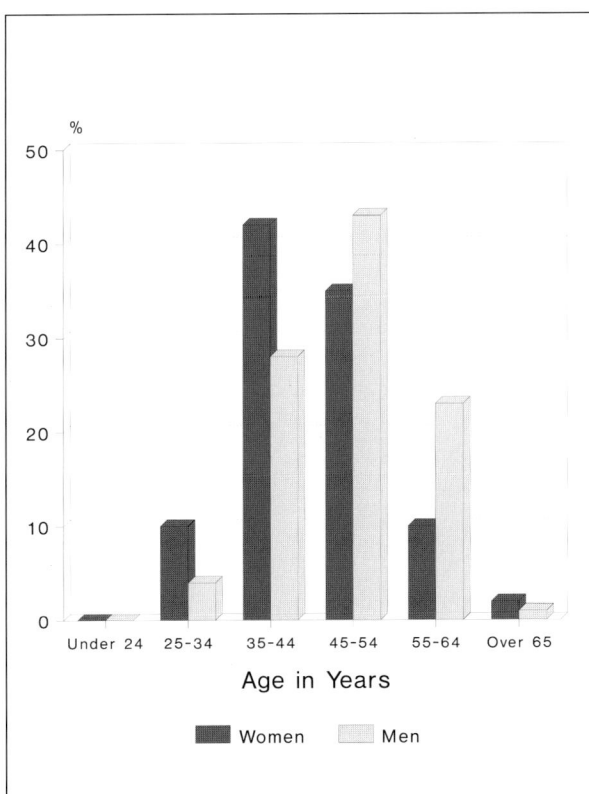

Fig 4 - Relationship between age and company ownership

Management function

Overall, women managers are still more likely to work in administrative functions or in the public sector than their male counterparts. 15 per cent of

Organisation activity

The differences between the two 1992 samples are equally marked in relation to employing organisation. 18 per cent of men work in an organisation devoted to manufacturing or production, compared to only 8 per cent of women. By contrast, 22 per cent of women work for an organisation whose main function is education or training, compared to only 10 per cent of men.

Main activity of organisation

	Women %	Men %
Education/training	22	10
Professional/scientific/consultancy	14	14
Public administration/government	14	12
Other	14	11
Manufacturing/production	8	18
Financial services	7	7
Retail/distribution/transport	5	6
Other services	5	3
Utilities	3	5
Marketing/sales/advertising	3	2
Construction/engineering	3	10
Leisure	2	2

The changes in the management function of women managers since 1989 are reflected in changes of employing organisation. The proportion of those working in public administration/government has increased from 11 to 14 per cent and of those in education and training from 16 to 22 per cent.

It is not clear why these proportions have risen. Some of the variations may reflect recruitment patterns among the IM membership as a whole and may not be valid on a national scale. If they are indicative of a national trend, they are disturbing: despite the growth in equal opportunities policies, women IM members appear not to be reaching the top in functions or industries which have been traditionally dominated by men.

There is a notable public/private sector split between male and female managers. 36 per cent of women work in the public sector compared to 24 per cent of men. This may in part be because the public sector has traditionally done more to recruit and retain women managers: other research by IM shows, for example, that the public sector leads in the adoption of flexible working practices (6). The public sector may also be more rigorous in its approach to and adoption of equal opportunities legislation.

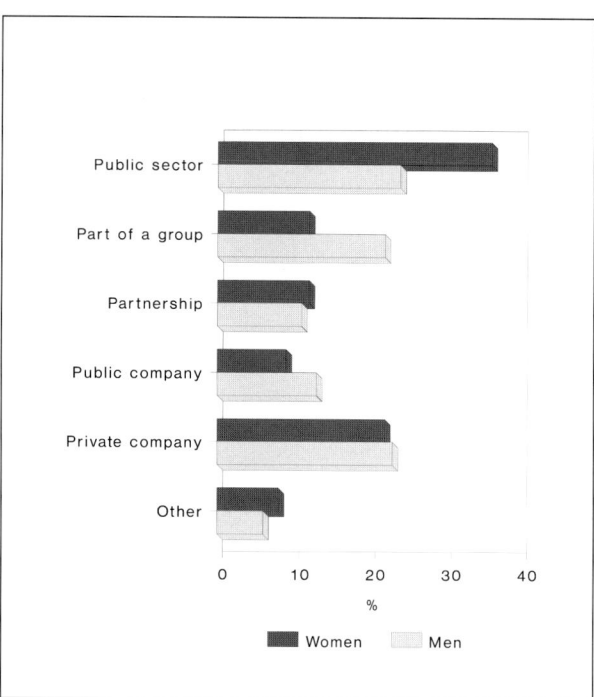

Fig 6 - Organisation sector

Size of company

The size of employing company is virtually identical for both men and women. Excluding those who run their own business, 50 per cent of women and 48 per cent of men work in a company with over 1,000 employees, while 4 per cent of women and 3 per cent of men work in a company with fewer than 10 employees.

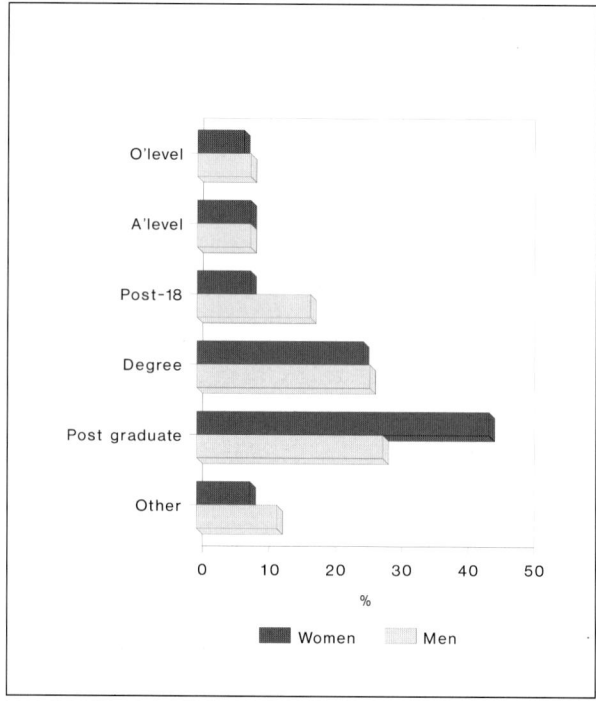

Fig 7 - Highest qualification

8

Qualifications

Significant differences emerge between the two samples in relation to educational attainment: overall, women IM members are better educated than their male counterparts: 44 per cent have a post-graduate or Masters degree or equivalent qualification, compared to 28 per cent of men. Details of other qualifications are shown below.

[IM members overall are more highly qualified than managers in general: a management qualification is one of the criteria for entry to membership].

Regional breakdown

The regional profile of the female IM membership as a whole (rather than of survey respondents) is shown below.

Regional breakdown of women managers

Region	%
Northern Ireland	3
Scotland	7
North West	8
North East	8
South Wales	2
West Midlands	6
East Midlands	6
Anglia	4
South West	3
West	10
Northern Home Counties	8
Greater London	22
Southern Counties	5
Southern England	8

[Source: IM membership data base]

Personal details

Respondents were asked about their personal circumstances in order to establish whether these had any effect on a career in management or on attitudes to women managers.

Marital status

92 per cent of male managers are married compared to only 68 per cent of their female colleagues. Women managers are more likely to be divorced or separated: 12 per cent against 5 per cent of men.

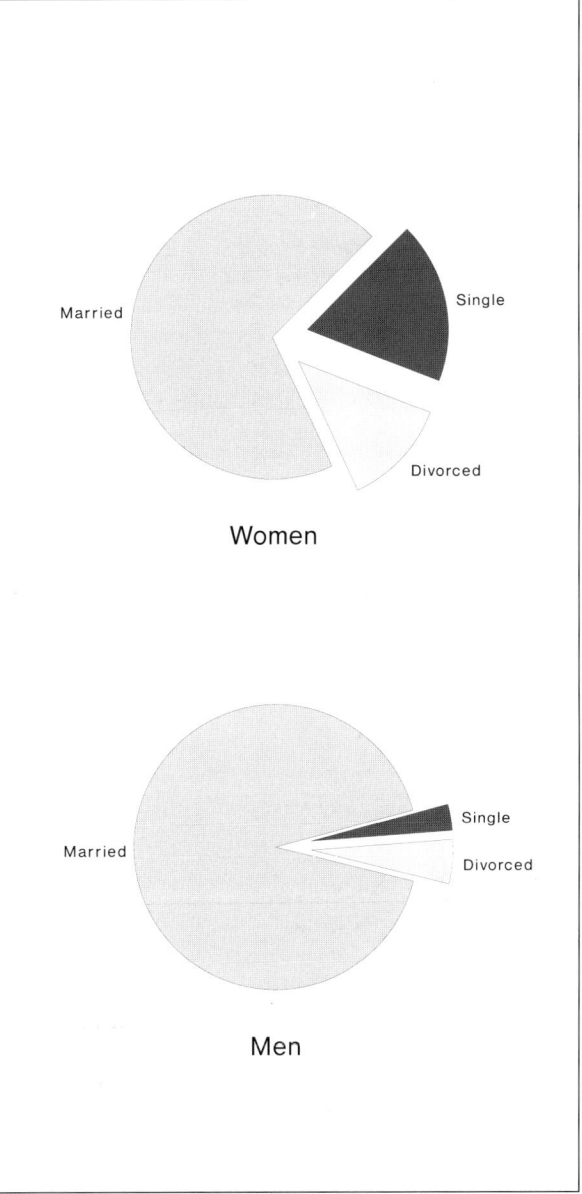

Fig 8 - Marital status

There has been a slight increase since 1989 in the proportion of married women managers. 61 per cent of respondents were married in 1989 against 38 per cent who were single: the 1989 survey did not ask about the numbers who were divorced/separated.

Household income

There are differences between the two samples in relation to income. We asked both male and female managers whether they contributed the principal or secondary income in their household. A third of women declined to answer this question: many volunteered the comment that both incomes were "equal" either in status or in numerical terms. Of the women who did respond, 64 per cent contributed the main household income, including 57 per cent of married women.

9

The same question was asked of male managers: 95 per cent contribute the principal income.

The results show a rise in the contribution of women. In 1989, 59 per cent of those responding described their salary as the principal one, while 44 per cent of married women contributed the main income.

These findings confirm a general upward trend in women's earnings power. The 1992 National Management Salary Survey (5) shows that while women still lag their male counterparts in absolute earnings power, the differential is narrowing. In the year to January 1992, female managers' earnings rose by 8 per cent against 6 per cent for men.

However, female managers still earn less on average than their male counterparts. The average women manager earns £25,054 a year against £29,945 for male managers.

Previous caring responsibilities

Both men and women managers were asked if they had - or had ever had - responsibilities for caring, whether for children or for elderly or disabled relatives. The responses reveal unexpected differences between the two samples.

Nearly half the women (48 per cent) say they have never had any caring responsibilities whereas only 12 per cent of men are in this position. Some of these differences are clearly attributable to differences in

marital status: 80 per cent of single women have never had a caring responsibility. Some of the differences may also be attributable to differing interpretations of 'responsibility'. For some men, this may be limited to providing financial support for the family, whereas women may be more likely to give it a wider interpretation.

Not all the differences can be explained in this way. Of the managers who are married, 86 per cent of men have had responsibility for children, compared to only 49 per cent of women. This difference cannot be attributed entirely to the age gap between the two samples: it is clear that many women managers, for whatever reason, are not combining children and a career in management.

Current caring responsibilities

There are also marked differences between the two samples in terms of current caring responsibilities. 63 per cent of women have no caring responsibilities at present, compared to only 30 per cent of men. Most of these differences are attributable to responsibilities for children. Women are again much less likely to have responsibility for children below school leaving age: 26 per cent of women currently have children below 16 compared to 62 per cent of men. Again, this difference can only be partly accounted for by age differences between the two samples.

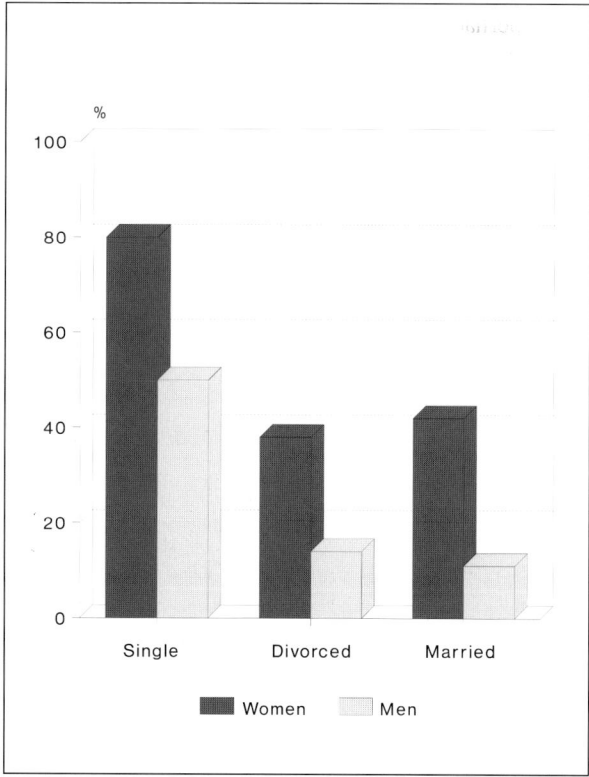

Fig 9 - Respondants who have never had a caring responsibility

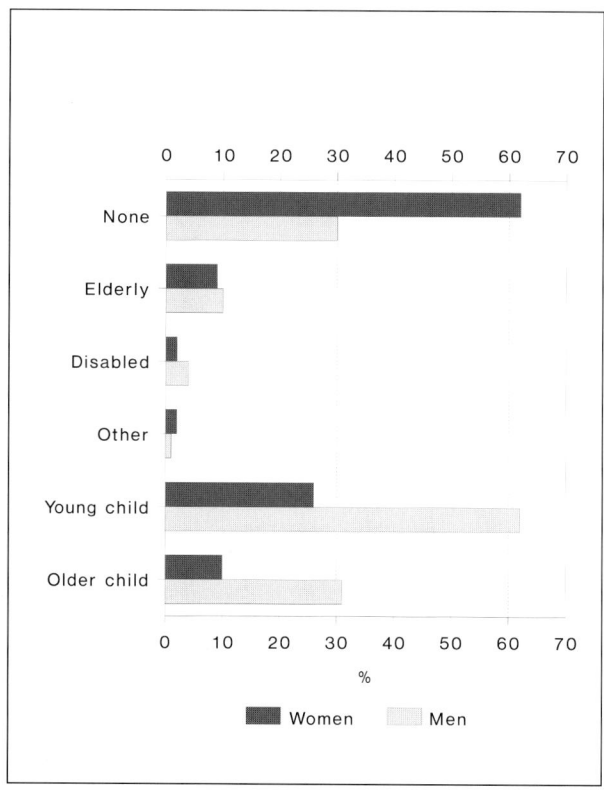

Fig 10 - Current caring responsibilities

Effect of caring responsibilities on a management career

Both the men and women managers who had had a caring responsibility were asked whether this had affected their career. The differences between the two samples are marked. While women managers are much less likely to have children, where they do so the impact on their career is much greater. 42 per cent of women managers say their career has been affected by a caring responsibility, while only 16 per cent of men believe that caring has had an adverse impact.

Further analysis of these results shows that children are perceived to have the greatest effect. 49 per cent of women managers who had children felt this had adversely affected their career, while 35 per cent of those who had cared for the elderly perceived an adverse effect and 33 per cent of those caring for the disabled.

Although the sample sizes are too small to draw firm conclusions, the pattern for male managers appears to be different. Of the men who had had caring responsibilities, those caring for the disabled were most likely to perceive an adverse impact: children were seen as much less disruptive to a male management career.

The proportion of men and women managers perceiving a benefit to their career from a caring responsibility are similar and surprisingly high. 12 per cent of women feel they have derived benefit from a caring responsibility against 15 per cent of men.

39 per cent of women feel that caring has had no effect at all on their career against 47 per cent of men. 23 per cent of male managers did not feel able to judge the effect of caring on their career, suggesting some ambivalence about the likely impact.

Can caring be combined with a management career?

Both men and women were asked whether they believed it was possible successfully to combine a career in management and a caring responsibility. The responses are remarkable for their similarity. In each case, 38 per cent replied in the affirmative, without any qualification. A slim majority in each case believed that the combination is possible only at 'considerable personal cost' - 51 per cent of men and 54 per cent of women. Respondents were not asked for a view on whether they believed that cost to be too high.

Only 3 per cent of women believed that it was not possible successfully to combine a caring responsibility and a management career. 7 per cent of men took this view, perhaps because a higher proportion of the men in this sample had a caring responsibility.

Is it possible successfully to combine a career in management and a caring responsibility?

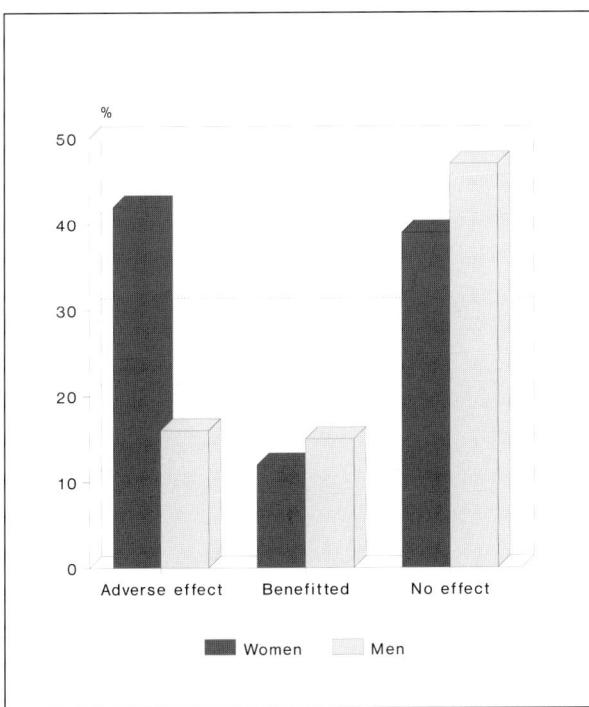

Fig 11 - Effect of caring responsibility on a management career

	Women %	Men %
Yes	38	38
Yes, but only at considerable personal cost	54	51
No	3	7

Women managers only were asked what the main reasons were for caring affecting their career. They were able to give up to three. Top of these was difficulty in working long hours (48 per cent) closely followed by the need to work locally (45 per cent). Other reasons attracted reasonably low scores.

Main reasons why caring had adversely affected women's careers

	%
Difficulty in working long hours	48
Need to work locally	45
Considered not to be a career person	25
Difficulty in working standard office hours	21
Unable to travel	21
Considered potentially unreliable	11
Need to take frequent time off	7
Other	23

A large number of women perceived benefits to their career as a result of caring. The majority listed the ability to adopt a more balanced attitude to work as the main advantage (59 per cent) closely followed by the acquisition of better time management skills. 21 per cent felt that caring had given them the opportunity to acquire new skills, while 20 per cent felt that it had given them the opportunity to re-focus their career through training or a career break.

Career breaks

Women managers were asked whether they had ever taken a career break. *['Career break' was used in the sense of any prolonged period away from the employment market].* 57 per cent of women had had an uninterrupted career, while 29 per cent had taken a break for child care and 10 per cent for training. The remaining 9 per cent had taken a career break for a variety of reasons.

The time spent out of the employment market varied considerably. While 15 per cent of women had taken a break of under 6 months, 5 per cent had been out of the employment market for over 10 years in total. In general, the longer breaks were for child care. Of those who took a break for training, 35 per cent had been away for between six months and a year while a further 26 per cent had taken a 1-2 year break. For child care, the largest single majority of 28 per cent had taken a break of between 3 and 5 years.

The survey also confirms the findings of other research, that absence from employment often exerts downward pressure on a career. 35 per cent of women returned to work at a lower level, while 43 per cent returned at the same level. Only 22 per cent returned at a higher level. As one woman manager commented:

"If you leave work to have a child, you effectively lose all skills in the employer's eyes and have to start again."

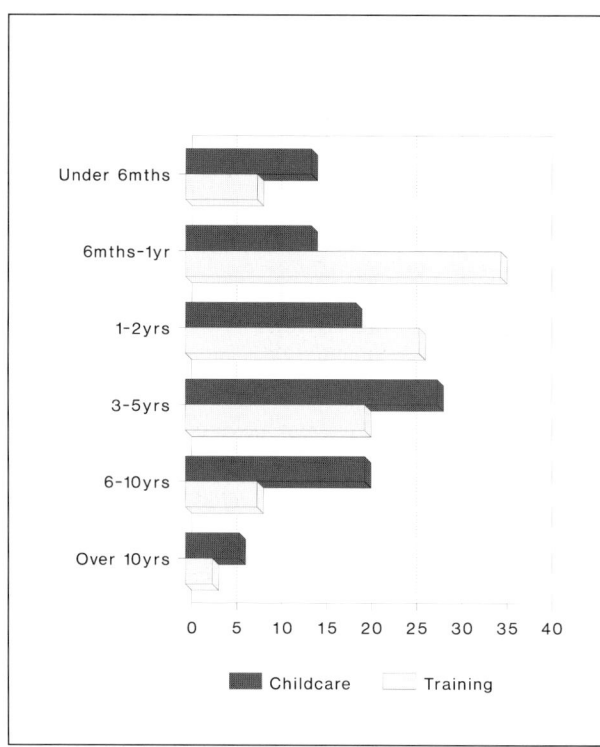

Fig 12 - Length of career breaks for child care and training

That perception is confirmed by the following comment from a male manager:

"If anyone takes a career break for any reason their knowledge of the business must slip and they should not expect to return at the same level."

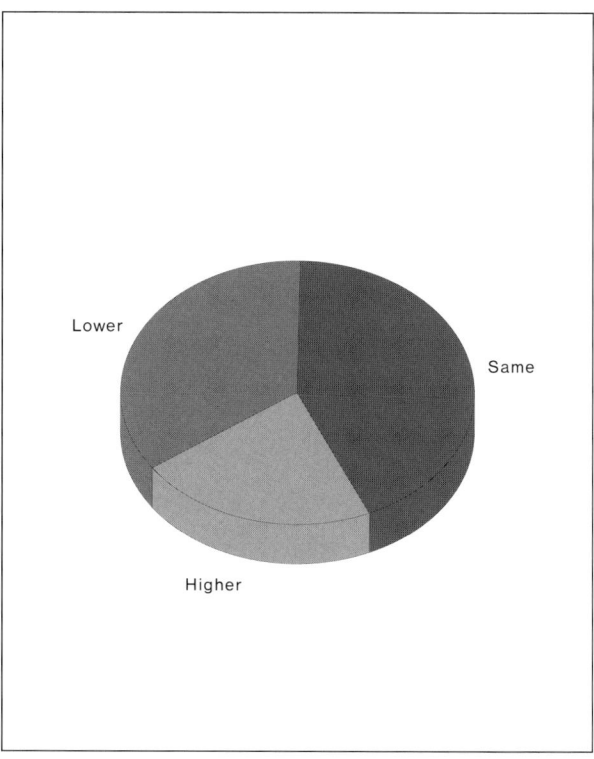

Fig 13 - Impact of career break on level of return

The reason for taking a career break has a significant impact on the level at which women return. Of those who had taken a break for training, 44 per cent returned at a higher level, compared to only 15 per cent of those who had taken a break for child care. Conversely, 39 per cent of those taking a break for child care returned at a lower level, with only 15 per cent returning at a higher level.

Career progression

Both men and women were asked how they anticipated their career developing. Only 8 per cent believed their career would now stagnate due to an invisible barrier within their organisation.

However, while women may not perceive or be aware of the existence of such a barrier, they are notably less optimistic than men about the prospects for promotion within their own organisation. Only 20 per cent of women anticipate an internal promotion as their next step, compared to 36 per cent of men. Does this reflect the continued existence of barriers or simply the desire of women managers for greater mobility between organisations?

Women, by contrast, were more optimistic than men about the prospects for promotion with another organisation. 20 per cent foresaw this as their next career move, compared to 14 per cent of men. Other career moves attracted equal votes from both men and women - with the exception of retirement as the final move. No less than a quarter of men are anticipating retirement (or equivalent) compared to 10 per cent of women. This largely reflects the older age profile of the male managers.

For both men and women age is clearly a key factor, but the patterns are different. Both men and women between 25 and 34 perceive promotion within their own organisation as the most likely step, but the proportions vary: 35 per cent for women and 53 per cent for men. These proportions fall to 30 per cent and 48 per cent between 35 and 44 and to 22 per cent and 36 per cent for the next decade.

The findings on career progression can be compared with previous BIM research on the expectations of middle managers. A 1992 BIM report analysed the career moves of over 1,000 BIM members at middle management level (7). The sample was predominantly male. 54 per cent of those questioned thought that their next move would be upwards, while 14 per cent anticipated a sideways move. The respondents to this survey, conducted in 1991, were much more optimistic than respondents to the current survey - perhaps because they had not yet realised the extent to which the recession is affecting managerial jobs.

Barriers to Women in Management

A number of questions were asked only of the women managers about the barriers they had experienced in their career to date.

Women were asked first to give details of any barriers they had encountered. The existence of a 'men's club' network attracted the highest vote (43 per cent). As one woman manager commented:

> "Old Boys Networks are alive and strong."

This was followed by prejudice from colleagues (35 per cent), lack of career guidance (28 per cent) and sexual discrimination or harassment (23 per cent). These attitudinal barriers were all perceived as greater obstacles than some of the physical barriers which have traditionally been seen as barring the progress of women. According to one woman:

> "The provision of child care is of little use to women wishing to progress in business as it is ultimately up to men to appoint."

19 per cent of the sample said they had encountered no barriers in their career to date. Managerial level had a significant impact on responses to this question. 34 per cent of those describing themselves as chairmen, 24 per cent of directors and 23 per cent of senior managers say they have encountered no barriers, against only 11 per cent of middle managers.

In the same way, the prejudice of colleagues is perceived as a greater barrier, the lower women are in the management ladder. 45 per cent of junior managers rate it as significant compared to 33 per cent of directors and 35 per cent of chairmen. This does not apply though to the old boys network which is viewed as the major obstacle at every level of management. Perceptions of barriers decline with age as they do with rank - the two are obviously linked. 42 per cent of 25-34 year olds list prejudice as a barrier compared to 33 per cent of those between 45 and 54 and 27 per cent of those between 55 and 64 (small sample).

Marital status also appears to have some bearing on perceptions of barriers, although in somewhat unexpected ways. Both divorced and single women are more likely to rate prejudice as a barrier than their married counterparts - 41 per cent against 33 per cent. This is doubtless explicable by the lack of other physical barriers encountered by single women (e.g., lack of child care). But there was no obligation on respondents to list non-existent barriers and it is significant that so many divorced and single women volunteered prejudice as a barrier.

In the same way, perceptions are affected by caring responsibilities. The differences here were less marked but still noteworthy. Those without responsibilities were more likely to rate prejudice as a barrier. This may again be because prejudice assumes greater importance in the absence of other tangible difficulties such as child care problems or inflexible working patterns.

Many married women might be surprised by these findings. As one commented:

> "Once you've had a child, your're automatically regarded as less efficient, regardless of evidence to the contrary".

Which is the greatest barrier to women in management?

Women managers were then asked which barrier they viewed as the single biggest obstacle. Again, the existence of a men's club attracted the highest score. 23 per cent of respondents perceived this as the biggest single barrier to the progress of their career. No other obstacle attracted a significant response. The proportion who perceive no barriers fell slightly in the response to this question, to 17 per cent. Beyond that, family commitments and lack of confidence/motivation attracted responses of 10 per cent, while 9 per cent viewed prejudice of male colleagues as the biggest barrier.

Which barriers have women encountered in their career - and which is the single biggest barrier

	Barriers in career %	Single biggest barrier %
'Mens club' network	43	23
Prejudice of colleagues	35	9
Lack of career guidance	28	7
Sexual discrimination/ harassment	23	5
Lack of training provision	18	3
Lack of personal motivation/ confidence	18	10
Family commitments	17	10
Inflexible working patterns	12	4
Social pressure [e.g. from friends, parents]	12	1
Lack of adequate childcare	9	3
Insufficient education	7	3
No barriers	19	17
Other	9	6

Support

Women managers only were asked from whom they had received support in their careers. 80 per cent of women had received positive support from partners/family, while 49 per cent had received support from a male boss and 16 per cent support from a female boss. 47 per cent had received support from colleagues. Very few had been supported by employers - only 15 per cent - and role models, whether male or female, were not generally seen as providing help. Only 14 per cent had received support from a women's network or support group. Given the dearth of senior women in management, the proportion of this sample receiving support from a woman boss is very high.

Women respondents were then asked which had been of most help during their career. 53 per cent said they had received most help from partners or family and 17 per cent from a male boss. 10 per cent of women had received most support from colleagues, while only 3 per cent had received the most help from their employer.

From whom have women managers received positive support - and who has provided most support?

	Positive support %	Most support %
Partner/family	80	53
Colleagues	47	10
Male boss	49	17
Female boss	16	3
Male role model	12	4
Female role model	13	2
Employer	15	3
Women's network/ suppor t group	14	3
Other 8	8	

These results were cross-analysed by marital status. Even those who were single or divorced said they had received most support from family or partner, followed by male boss or colleagues. In every case, employers came near the bottom of the list.

Despite the extent of support from female bosses, many women were critical of senior women managers. One commented:

"Women who make it to the top do not help or mentor others to do likewise."

Another that:

"The attitude of certain women in business does more harm than any man ever could."

Respect for women managers

Women managers only were asked whether they feel they receive adequate respect as a woman manager from staff, colleagues and superiors, both male and female. The general picture is one of widespread respect for women in management roles, but there are some disturbing exceptions. Only two thirds of women managers feel they receive adequate respect from male superiors and only 70 per cent from female superiors. Female colleagues and staff are in general seen as affording more respect to women managers than their male counterparts. As one woman manager in a large company noted:

"There is a subtle way in which we are never given quite the full authority, never quite the full credit, never quite the full respect."

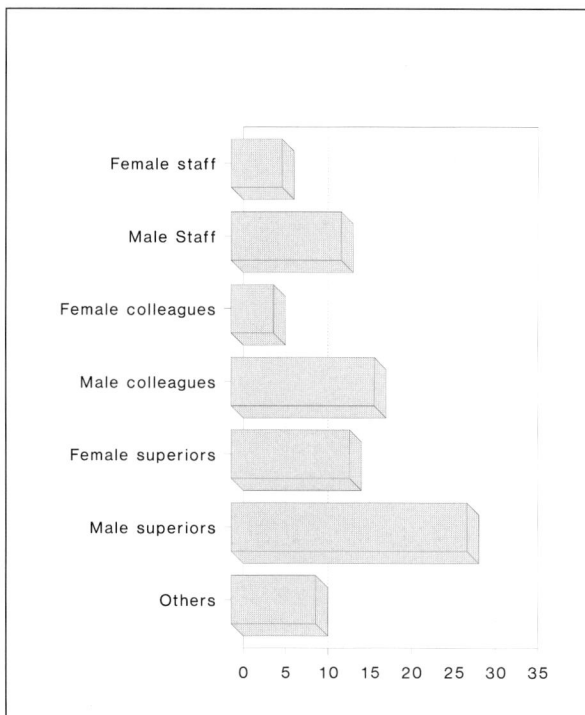

Fig 14 - Those not showing respect to women managers

The chart categories from top to bottom: Female staff, Male Staff, Female colleagues, Male colleagues, Female superiors, Male superiors, Others. Axis: 0 5 10 15 20 25 30 35

The role of women in management

Both men and women managers were asked how far they agreed with a series of attitude statements about the role of women in management. The responses again reveal some differences between the two samples.

Skills of women managers

The most significant differences relates to views about the skills of women managers. While 74 per cent of women 'strongly agree' that they bring positive skills to the workplace, this view is shared by only 35 per cent of male managers. One male manager took the view:

> *"In general women do not make good managers - although they have much to offer in the work-place."*

In total, 99 per cent of women agree or strongly agree that women contribute positive skills, while 94 per cent of men are of this view.

Management careers for women

Differences also emerge about attitudes to management careers for women. While 50 per cent of women 'strongly disagreed' with the statement that women should not combine a management career and motherhood, only 26 per cent of men strongly disagreed with this statement.

It is useful to compare this finding with research on general attitudes to women's place at work. In a Reader's Digest/MORI poll on the family (8). 45 per cent of respondents agreed or strongly agreed that: "women with young children should not go out to work."

Many of the men expressed strong views about women as managers, which indicate the height of some of the remaining attitudinal barriers. These included:

> *"Successful management requires commitment with no outside worries - for women to succeed they must therefore be single or have adult children."*

Attitude to women managers

Both men and women managers were asked about the overall attitude to women managers from within their own organisation; from within their organisation's field of activity; and from within their own management function. The results again paint a picture of overall support, but with some qualifications.

Male managers have a slightly more positive view overall of others' attitudes to women managers, but the differences between the two samples are not significant. Both men and women managers are more positive about attitudes within their own organisation or their own function than they are about attitudes within their field of activity. One woman manager observed:

> *"Clients can be a worse problem than colleagues as there are fewer avenues of complaint."*

Respondents were asked what was the overall attitude to women managers from others within a. their own organisation, b. their organisation's field of activity and c. their own management function.

	Very Positive		Positive		Adequate		Negative		Very Negative	
Organisation	Women	27	Women	31	Women	29	Women	11	Women	2
	Men	19	Men	46	Men	25	Men	9	Men	2
Field of activity	Women	15	Women	33	Women	36	Women	14	Women	2
	Men	15	Men	41	Men	31	Men	12	Men	2
Function	Women	21	Women	38	Women	33	Women	7	Women	1
	Men	21	Men	44	Men	26	Men	8	Men	2

"With massive unemployment we don't need to encourage women into the work-place when they already have a role as a mother."

One woman manager took the view that:

" Culture still sees women as having jobs rather than careers."

Another commented [in relation to perceptions of women who combine marriage and management] that:

"... until public opinion changes, women will still be regarded as the main and uncaring parent."

Differences between men and women managers

Other differences of view were less significant. There was a sharp and interesting divergence about whether women managers are different to men in the work-place. 50 per cent of women and 58 per cent of men agreed or strongly agreed that women managers are no different to men, while 50 per cent of women and 42 per cent of men disagreed.

"Men and women are biologically different and so therefore are their management styles - different, not better/worse."

"Women no more offer different skills than men do - not all men are tough and not all women are caring. We are all different - hard and soft."

Should there be positive discrimination?

Positive discrimination is currently illegal, although positive action is allowed - eg, special training, to redress an existing imbalance in the work-force. There was little support among men or women for a change in the law. Only 1 per cent of men and 4 per cent of women strongly agree with positive discrimination, while 43 per cent of men and 29 per cent of women strongly disagreed.

The consensus among women seemed to be that:

"Women do not require positive discrimination, but if they are to continue playing a dual role, they do need assistance."

This was generally supported by men: one expressed the view that:

"Discrimination is wrong but women do need more encouragement and special training".

Should all managers receive equal treatment irrespective of family responsibilities?

There was strong support for the view that all managers should receive equal treatment, irrespective of their family responsibilities. Only 15 per cent of women disagreed with this view and 14 per cent of men. Support among women was marginally stronger; 49 per cent of women 'strongly agreed' with the view against 37 per cent of men.

Working for a woman manager

Women still have some way to go in being fully accepted in senior management positions. 18 per cent of men admitted that they find it difficult, or would find it difficult, to work for a woman manager - and 12 per cent of women made the same confession. At the same time, only 42 per cent of women 'strongly disagree' with this statement, the remainder disagreeing, against 53 per cent of men who disagree and 30 per cent who strongly disagree. As one woman commented:

"Men are happy to work with women and for women to be promoted provided they do not have to work under them."

Another queried:

"Why are women seen by men to be a greater threat than men?."

Respondents were asked for their opinion on the following statements:

	Strongly Agree %		Agree %		Disagree %		Strongly Disagree %	
Women have positive skills to bring to the workplace	Women	74	Women	25	Women	1	Women	0
	Men	35	Men	59	Men	5	Men	1
Women managers are not different to men in the workplace	Women	19	Women	31	Women	46	Women	4
	Men	15	Men	43	Men	37	Men	4
There should be positive discrimination for women managers	Women	4	Women	14	Women	54	Women	29
	Men	1	Men	7	Men	48	Men	43
Women should not combine a management career and motherhood	Women	2	Women	5	Women	43	Women	50
	Men	6	Men	15	Men	54	Men	26
All managers should receive equatreatment, irrespective of their family responsibilities	Women	49	Women	36	Women	12	Women	3
	Men	37	Men	49	Men	13	Men	1
I do find it/would find it difficult to work for a senior woman manager	Women	5	Women	7	Women	46	Women	42
	Mwn	4	Men	14	Men	53	Men	30

Government support

Both men and women managers were asked for views on the extent of support that should be provided by government.

Support for child care

Women and men expressed similar views about the need for further government support. 55 per cent of women and 59 per cent of men believed that tax relief should be extended to all employer funded creches, while 48 per cent of women and 46 per cent of men believed there should be tax exemption for all employer funded child care.

There was greater support among women for the extension of tax relief to all forms of child care. 64 per cent were in favour, against 41 per cent of men.

There was also greater support among women for the belief that government should provide assistance with after school care provision: 56 per cent of women supported this view against 31 per cent of men.

Support for an extension of the statutory period of maternity leave was lukewarm among both men and women. Only 20 per cent of men were in favour and 31 per cent of women. There was greater support for paternity leave, - although women managers were generally more enthusiastic than men. 43 per cent were in favour, against 27 per cent of men.

There was little overall support for government assistance for specific training for women although a significant minority of both men and women were in favour - 27 per cent of women, 19 per cent of men.

Only 6 per cent of women believe that the government should provide no assistance at all. The figure rises to 16 per cent for men.

Respondents were asked which of the following forms of assistance they believed the government should provide.

	Women %	Men %
Tax relief for all employer funded creches	55	59
Tax exemption on all employer funded childcare	48	46
Tax relief for all forms of childcare	64	41
After school care provision	56	31
More lenient maternity leave	31	20
More lenient paternity leave	43	27
Tax relief for all carers	64	42
Specific training for women	27	19
Other	5	2
No assistance	6	16

A comparison of views on what organisations should be providing, compared to government, shows that in the area of creche facilities, assistance for carers, training and after school provision, there is stronger support for provision by government. They are generally perceived as having a greater responsibility than organisations.

Working patterns

Respondents were asked about the different working patterns offered by their organisation. The most commonly available is part time work, but it was not clear whether this option was always available at management level. Only 3 per cent of women managers currently work part time (defined as under 30 hours a week).

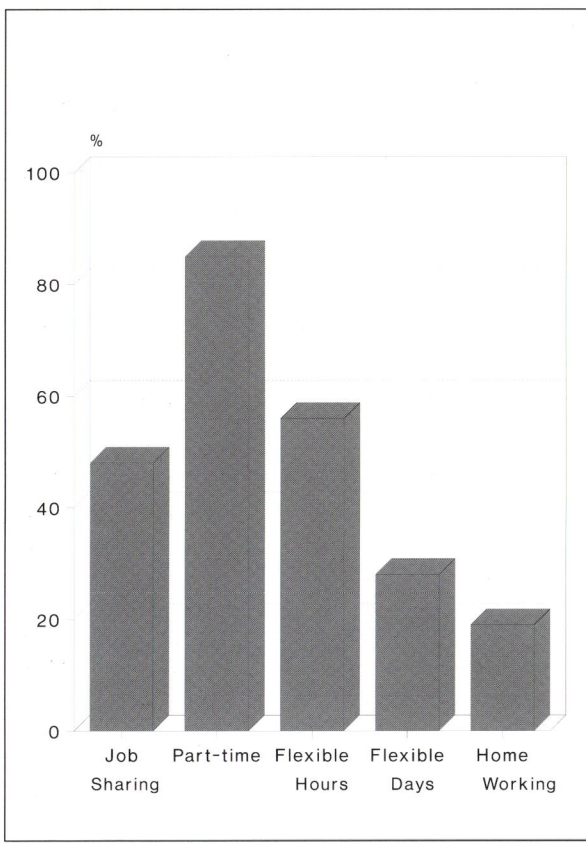

%

100

80

60

40

20

0

| Job Sharing | Part-time | Flexible Hours | Flexible Days | Home Working |

Fig 15 - Flexible working patterns

56 per cent of organisations offer flexible work (hours per day) and 28 per cent flexible work in days per year. 48 per cent offer job sharing but only 19 per cent working mainly from home. Again it is not clear how far these options are available at management level. Only 1 per cent of the women in this sample work flexible hours. None are sharing jobs.

The low level of flexible working is largely attributable to the continuing [male] belief that management needs to be a (very) full-time job. One male manager took the view that:

> "Management requires total dedication - this cannot be given by part-timers of either sex."

Conversely, women called for changes in company attitudes.

> "It is time that the British working culture changed to recognise performance in terms of achieved targets rather than compliance with company culture."

There are few differences between organisations in relation to the types of flexible working offered. The exception is for job sharing, where 80 per cent of the women working for 'government' report that this is available, against an average of 48 per cent. This finding is confirmed by a public/private sector split of results in this area. In every case bar one, the public sector is ahead of its private sector counterparts in the amount and type of flexible working offered.

Organisational support

Both men and women managers were asked about the support offered by their organisation; and for their views on what their organisation should provide. In relation to the needs of women managers, there are significant gaps between what is on offer and what women feel is needed - although some of these may reflect a degree of under-reporting by women who do not currently have child care responsibilities.

Respondents were asked whether their organisation provided, and whether they thought it should provide, the following assistance:

	Does provide %		Should provide %	
	Women	Men	Women	Men
Creche for children on site	21	11	35	30
Creche for children off site	11	7	38	38
Links with local social services	28	35	39	37
Monetary assistance with childcare	9	7	43	33
Other assistance with childcare	7	8	41	35
After school care provision	3	3	36	35
Assistance for carers	6	13	49	37
Special training for women	37	34	33	31
Quotas for women in management	9	10	25	15
No assistance	26	35	5	12

Overall, few organisations are providing positive help for their women managers - or for carers in general. The most common form of help that is given is special training for women which 37 per cent of women say their organisation provides. This is the only area in which provision exceeds expectations: only 33 per cent of women believe their organisation should give them special training.

Beyond training, provision by employers is patchy. 21 per cent of women say their organisation provides a creche on site and 11 per cent a creche off site. This compares to 11 per cent of men who have access to a creche on site and 7 per cent who have access to an off-site creche. *[These figures are all much higher than the national average: there are only 3,000 employers' creches nation-wide and only three per cent of employees have access to one].*

It is not clear why the proportions are much higher for woman managers. It is possible that employers are more likely to provide facilities for managers than for other employees; or that women managers more likely to be drawn to, or remain with, organisations which offer assistance. The figures may also indicate the high proportion of women managers who work in national or local government. This sector has traditionally offered better child care provision than private industry, partly as a way of recruiting and retaining women managers.

More women - 28 per cent - say their organisation offers links with local social services, while only 9 per cent say their organisation gives monetary help with child care, such as vouchers. 7 per cent of women say their organisation offers other assistance for child care. The figures are similar for male respondents. In these areas, there may be some under-reporting: most employees will know whether or not their company has a creche, but unless they currently have children may not be aware of less visible forms of help.

One of the largest gaps between provision and expectation is in the area of out of school care. Only 3 per cent of women say their organisation offers any help yet 36 per cent would like support in this area. Even more feel strongly about the lack of support for carers. Only six per cent of women say their organisation provides assistance - but 49 per cent would like to see some form of help.

This reflects a general view among both men and women that the needs of carers are not sufficiently recognised. Many men and women volunteered the comment that "too much is done" for women with children while the needs of those caring for elderly or disabled relatives are ignored.

One male manager commented:

"The money, time and stress of caring for a disabled relative is ignored";

while a female manager said:

"You choose to marry and have children - you do not choose to be a carer, society pressure forces it on you."

Quotas for women in management are currently illegal, although targets are permissible. Unsurprisingly, there is little support among respondents for any form of quota. Only 25 per cent of women and 15 per cent of men believe that their organisation should provide quotas while 69 per cent believe they should not: the remainder had no view. Against these figures, only nine per cent women and ten per cent of men say their organisation provides quotas [these are presumably 'targets' rather than 'quotas', but the perception of them is interesting].

26 per cent of women and 35 per cent of men say their organisation provides no assistance. It is not clear whether the differences between the two samples reflect a reduced awareness among men of the support available for women, or a tendency for women to be drawn toward organisations which are perceived as more supportive.

The views of both men and women on what their organisations should provide are fairly similar, although women are more likely to feel that their organisation has a responsibility to provide support. Many respondents, men in particular, highlighted the difficulties for small organisations in providing generous maternity leave or child care facilities. Some also took the view that it was not the job of the organisation to provide help to employees:

"Companies are designed to make a profit and provide a service to customers - not to provide extras for staff."

Conclusions

Are women in the wrong management jobs?

The results of this survey reveal superficial similarities in the profiles of male and female IM members. Within each sample the proportions of men and women at junior, middle and senior grades are very similar. Both samples also work for similar sized companies and the proportions of those running their own business are virtually identical. Few clues there to the lack of women in management positions in general.

Where differences begin to emerge is in relation to management function and organisation activity. Women are much more likely to be in education or training, administration or government: only 1 per cent are in a manufacturing or production function.

These figures provide one of the first clues to the dearth of women in management. If they are typical of women managers in general, it is not surprising there are so few women in senior positions. Many women are simply in the wrong function or in the wrong industry if they want to make it to the top. Their position is like that of the traveller who on asking his way was told: 'Well, I wouldn't start from here'.

This dilemma was highlighted by NEDO in its 1990 report (4) and by the Institute of Manpower Studies in work commissioned by NEDO (9). Both point out that women make early career choices which can disqualify them from senior management positions. They are often concentrated in support sectors, such as market research, from where it is difficult to move to a mainstream career; or in support functions, such as personnel or administration, which are not perceived as providing the 'business' experience necessary for a senior role. Either way, women can be knocked off the management ladder at an early stage.

Why do women enter support functions?

What is not clear is how far women are entering support functions through choice, or how far their selection is still determined by social and cultural conditioning. Their career may be decided by education choices made at an early age. Women are much less likely to take science subjects at GCSE/A

level: boys outnumber girls 4 to 1 in entries to A level physics; and to take business related degrees: only 20 per cent of taught higher degrees in business and management are taken by women (10).

Against this background, it is significant that lack of career guidance was perceived by many women as one of the major barriers to women in management. It is beyond the remit of this report to look at the reasons behind early career choices; but it is clear that considerable work needs to be done at the level of secondary and further/higher education to ensure that women are not discouraged at the first hurdle from pursuing 'male' careers.

While public action on education and career choices is needed in the long term, the findings also have immediate significance for corporate policies. They confirm that many of the recognised routes to the top are still effectively closed to women through their early career selection. This has profound implications for equal opportunities policies. If organisations are serious about increasing the proportion of women in management, they need to look as closely at the functional distribution of their women employees as at their management level. If women are still largely concentrated in the support functions, any policy aimed at increasing the proportion of women managers is unlikely to succeed without a radical re-appraisal of the career path needed to reach the top.

Women and the public sector

We are also unlikely to see equal proportions of male and female company directors, as long as women continue to favour the public sector. The reasons for this preference are diverse. Because they have not kept pace in the past with private sector salary levels, public sector employers have offered better terms and conditions in other areas such as flexible working arrangements in order to attract and retain good candidates. In its role of public model, the public sector has also been more scrupulous in its observance of equal opportunities legislation. As a result, it has probably been perceived as more sympathetic to women managers.

Yet despite its family friendly appearance, the public sector has been little more successful in promoting women: they account for only 4 per cent of those in senior grades in the civil service. This appears to show that, despite its significance, being in the wrong job is only one of the hurdles. Even when they are competing on similar terms, as in the civil service, women are not being promoted to senior positions in management.

The barriers to women in management

According to this sample, the biggest single barrier to the progress of women in management is the existence of the men's club network. While the sample may not be fully representative of female managers as a whole, it does provide the largest and most authoritative picture to date of senior women managers in Britain. Divorced and single women were more likely than their married colleagues to rate the men's club as a barrier. This suggests that much of the prejudice is against women per se, rather than being based on an assessment that women with children may not be capable of fulfilling a dual role.

These women's perceptions of the barriers are borne out by the responses of their male colleagues to statements about the role of women in management. If only a third of men strongly agree that women have positive skills to bring to the work-place, is it surprising that they are not appointing women to senior management positions? Even more revealing are the unprompted comments made by senior male managers. How many share the view that:

> *"With massive unemployment we don't need to encourage women into the work-place."*

Management is a male job

It is not only male attitudes that work against women. The received view of management in general is of a very traditional, very full time job. Most organisations expect their managers to work long hours, to travel and to give total commitment. Only 3 per cent of this sample of women work part time and only 1 per cent have flexible hours. Compare these to the national figures: in non-management jobs, 45 per cent of women work part-time (10).

Many management jobs still appear to be designed around the assumption that the managers will have a full time spouse to shoulder domestic responsibilities, a perception still shared by many male managers themselves. One took the view that:

> *"Successful management requires total commitment with no outside worries",*

another that

> *"Management requires total dedication - this cannot be given by part-timers of either sex".*

Are marriage and management incompatible?

This expectation of a management career, combined with the traditional responsibility of women for looking after home / family, has clearly defeated many women managers. For whatever reason, a significant minority within this sample have decided that management and marriage are incompatible. A third are unmarried and only half have had children. By contrast, 92 per cent of male managers are married and 86 per cent have had children.

We did not explore in the questionnaire the reasons why so many women did not have a family. It is possible that some had made a deliberate choice at an early stage, and that that choice has in itself made it easier for them to follow a management career. It is also possible that, faced with the practical difficulties of combining the two, many have elected for a career over children.

If the choice is a deliberate one for many, the findings seem to show that in the current corporate climate women are justified in making it if they do want to reach the top. Of the women managers who have had children, half say that caring has adversely affected their career. Similarly, 39 per cent of those who had taken a break to care for children had returned to work at a lower level. It is clear that, whatever the rhetoric of equal opportunities, having children still exerts downward pressure on a management career for almost half of women managers.

The pressures against change

The corporate perception of a management career is reinforced by external pressures. Widespread restructuring has resulted in the loss of thousands of management jobs as organisations trim management layers. Combined with the effects of the current recession, this has led to widespread managerial redundancy. Many managers - both male and female - may currently be concerned about the possible loss of their job. In this climate, it is unsurprising that managers feel pressure to be visible, to work full-time, not to take a break from their career, for fear that their job may disappear in their absence. It is also unsurprising that so many men may be reluctant to admit women to the club when they perceive a shortfall of managerial jobs for men.

At the same time, the rate of change within companies speeds up each year. It is increasingly difficult for any employee to take a prolonged break from employment and to maintain their knowledge and experience - without support from their employer.

Why the current approach will not succeed

Against this background, it seems unlikely that the current approach of government and employers will provide a solution to increasing the proportion of women in management. While they are welcome, the provision of creche facilities or generous maternity leave are simply means of allowing women with family responsibilities to mould themselves to a traditional management structure. This means in practice that many women opt out of one of their two dual roles. A large proportion of this sample have chosen a management career over a family. This is not a realistic or sustainable solution for the majority of women looking for a career in management.

The need for real change

If women are genuinely to succeed, a fundamental redesign of management careers is needed rather than cosmetic measures. A change of culture is required from one where managers are judged by the amount of time spent at work to one where they are judged by their own results and by those of their staff. As one female manager commented:

> "It is time that the British working culture changed to recognise performance in terms of achieved targets rather than compliance with company culture."

Most managers already fulfil myriad roles during the working day. Many are unavailable to staff or customers through absence in meetings or travelling.

All managers effectively work part-time on any one project. Yet companies still seem unable to make the mental leap of imagination that would allow them to change the structure of their management jobs. Until they do so, they may get less than optimum performance from both men and women managers who are increasingly combining dual roles.

The pressures against change

So why are companies so reluctant to change? Part of the answer lies in the paucity of senior women managers. Most decisions at board level that affect company structure or practices are still taken by men. However enlightened they may be, they are unlikely to appreciate the practical and pyschological issues faced by the majority of women managers. It is also clear from this report, that although they may not admit it publicly, many see women managers as a threat to their own position and will resist any attempt to unlock the barriers.

Against this background, it is clear that many equal opportunities policies are unlikely to be fully successful. Without a fundamental change to company attitudes, the setting of targets for women in management or the provision of creche facilities can even be counter-productive. Such measures can simply fuel resentment among male colleagues who believe that too much is being done to help women who should not be in a management position anyway. If it is to succeed, any policy designed to increase the proportion of women in management needs to be built around a re-design of the management career so that results are measured by targets achieved rather than compliance with company culture.

Recommendations

The following recommendations are aimed at employers and senior managers. Their aim is not to set out a checklist for the adoption of an equal opportunities policy: several bodies have already done this effectively, including NEDO in its 1990 report (4).

Instead, the recommendations highlight possible gaps in current policies. Many organisations assume that to lower the barriers to women in management, they should focus on practical ways of supporting women's needs. This report shows that while such support is welcome, it fails to tackle the real hurdle: that of male attitudes toward management. A policy targeted only at the perceived needs of women (e.g., special training, creche facilities) is unlikely to succeed in its aim of increasing the proportion of women in management, if it is implemented in a predominantly male culture. An equal opportunities policy should be part of a wider culture change programme.

The following recommendations set out the elements of the programme to be adopted by any company which is serious in its commitment to equal opportunities. They are illustrated by extracts from the policies of some of the few organisations who have adopted a holistic approach and considered the need to educate the work force as a whole rather than providing for women in isolation.

As the Midland Bank's policy spells out:

[Equal opportunities are about removing bias, prejudice and stereotyping so that the only acceptable form of discrimination is on the basis of ability].

The management career

Ensure that new entrants to your organisation receive career counselling and are not sidelined in administrative or support functions.

Carry out an audit of the representation of women in different functions as well as at different levels in the organisation. Follow it up with regular monitoring.

[The BBC systematically monitors both its work force and recruitment patterns to identify where blockages occur for women and areas where they are under-represented].

Reappraise your selection criteria for senior posts. Ensure they include a spread of experience which is not wholly male oriented.

Review the recruitment and selection criteria for all management posts up to and including board level. How far do they assume a traditional male career pattern or conjure up the image of a male manager? Use external advice to change them.

Look at your development and succession policies. Remove age limits or any unnecessary criteria to ensure that women who have taken career breaks or are late entrants to the work force are eligible for all management schemes.

Ensure all training and development courses are accessible to women. Hours and location are critical.

Remove the stigma attached to maternity leave or career breaks by making breaks available to all employees. Encourage men to use them.

[British Gas have introduced a scheme which allows all employees a career break of up to two years with an appropriate job on return]

Ensure that women on a career break do not suffer downward mobility. Keep in touch and provide training and updating.

The design of managers' jobs

Carry out a functional review of your management jobs. Which could be split or done part-time?

What is the scope for flexible working. Do all your managers need to be available first thing in the morning and last thing at night?

Review your communications systems. How much could technology improve the productivity of your managers?

Consider the scope for home working among all managerial and professional staff. Any managerial job which involves extended report writing or desk research can usually be completed more effectively away from the office.

[BT are conducting an experiment with directory assistance operators to investigate the technical, social and managerial aspects of tele-working].

Organisation culture

Recognise that prejudice exists in every organisation. Identify it in your own and act on it.

[The Bank of Scotland's policy recognises that:

Many people do not believe that they discriminate but in fact everyone has personal prejudices of one sort or another. These prejudices are largely unconscious and rarely deliberate].

Survey your own women managers and employees and find out where the barriers are in your own organisation - they may be unexpected. Make clear that the responsibility for eliminating prejudice rests with every employee.

[Midland Bank's policy makes clear that:

We all have a responsibility to ensure that our behaviour at work is not unfairly discriminatory. Putting an equal opportunities policy into practice is the responsibility of every employee, but particularly so for managers.]

Review your meetings culture. Are meetings structured and productive, with detailed action points? Discourage 'out of hours' meetings except in real emergencies.

Review the decision making process. Ensure it is transparent, open and accessible to all managers. Are informal networks or dinners to take the 'real decisions' really necessary?

Encourage a high performance culture based on results rather than time served. Change the appraisal criteria for managers to reflect this.

Introduce training programmes for all employees and managers to demonstrate the existence of prejudice and the steps needed to reduce it. This is as necessary as special training for women.

Don't set targets until and unless you have an effective culture change programme in place. Setting them in isolation can be counter- productive.

Home and management

Recognise, accept and be positive about caring responsibilities. Make clear that you view caring as the responsibility of all employees, not just women. Don't target child care support or provision only at women.

Be flexible. Don't assume that all women are caring for children. Review your benefits scheme and allow choice. Support for child care or for looking after an elderly relative may be more valuable to some employees than a company car.

References

1. Institute of Employment Research [1988], Review of the Economy and Employment, Occupational Update 1988. University of Warwick.

2. IMS Report No.224 "Family Friendly Working: New Hope or Old Hype" July 1992

3. BIM Survey of Women Mangers, by Tim Rycroft, 1989.

4. National Economic Development Office "Women Managers: The Untapped Resource". November 1990.

5. BIM/Remuneration Economics National Management Salary Survey 1992.

6. BIM/Manpower Survey of Long Term Employment Policies. July 1992.

7. "The Future of Middle Management", by Malcolm Wheatley. BIM, 1992.

8. Readers's Digest/MORI Poll "The British Family: A Survey of Public Attitudes", September 1991.

9. IMS Paper No.158 "Women into Management: Issues Influencing the Entry of Women into Managerial Jobs". IMS, 1990.

10. Labour Force Survey 1992.

Reading List

TITLE: Womanpower: Managing in Times of Demographic Turbulence
AUTHOR U Sekaran, F Leong
PUBLISHER: Newbury Park Calif, Sage, 1992

TITLE: Developing Women Through Training: A Practical Handbook
AUTHOR: L Willis, J Daisley
PUBLISHER: London, McGraw Hill, 1992

TITLE: Women Mean Business: A Practical Guide for Women Returners
AUTHOR: C Bamford, C McCarthy
PUBLISHER: London, BBC Books, 1991

TITLE A Chance for the Top
AUTHOR: C Dix
PUBLISHER: London, Bantam Press, 1990

TITLE: Women Managers: The Untapped Resource
AUTHOR: National Economic Development Office
PUBLISHER: London, Kogan Page, 1990

TITLE: Women in the Workforce: The Effects of Demographic Changes in the 1990's
AUTHOR: G Nevill
PUBLISHER: London, Industrial Society Press, 1990

TITLE: Returning to Work: A Directory of Education and Training for Women
AUTHOR: Women Returners Network
PUBLISHER: London, Kogan Page, 1990

TITLE: Getting There Job Hunting for Women
AUTHOR: M Wallis
PUBLISHER: London, Kogan Page, 1990

TITLE: Women into Management: Issues Influencing the Entry of Women into Managerial Jobs
AUTHOR: W Hirsh, C Jackson
PUBLISHER: Brighton, Falmer, 1990

TITLE: The Report of the Hansard Society Commision on Women at the Top
AUTHOR: Hansard Society for Parliamentary Government
PUBLISHER: London, 1990

TITLE: Returning to Work: A Practical Guide for Women
AUTHOR: A Reed
PUBLISHER: London, Kogan Page, 1989

TITLE: Powder in the Board Room: Report of a Survey of Women on the Boards of Top UK Companies
AUTHOR: V Holton, J Rabbetts
PUBLISHER: Ashridge Management Research Group, 1989

TITLE: Women in the World of Work: Statistical Analysis and Projections to the Year 2000
AUTHOR: S Nuss, E Denti, D Viry
PUBLISHER: Geneva, ILO, 1989

TITLE: Managing Two Careers: How to Survive as a Working Mother
AUTHOR: P O'Brien
PUBLISHER: London, Sheldon Press, 1989

TITLE: Survey of Women Managers: Interim Report
AUTHOR: T Rycroft
PUBLISHER: Corby, BIM, 1989

TITLE: Women Mean Business: A Successful and Survival Guide for the Woman Executive
AUTHOR: V Groocock
PUBLISHER: London, Ebury Press, 1988

TITLE: Women Managers: Changing Organisational Cultures
AUTHOR: G Asplund
PUBLISHER: Chichester, John Wiley, 1988

TITLE: The Competitive Woman
AUTHOR: J Cameron
PUBLISHER: London, Mercury Books, 1988

TITLE: Women at Work: Breaking Down the Barriers
AUTHOR: H Richardson, M J Davidson
PUBLISHER: Sheffield, MSC, 1987

TITLE: Flying High: The Womans Way to the Top
AUTHOR: L Jones
PUBLISHER: London, Fontana, 1987

TITLE: Moving Up: A Womans Guide to a Better Future at Work
AUTHOR: R Markel, C Faulder
PUBLISHER: London, Fontana, 1987

TITLE: Business Women: Present and Future
AUTHOR: D Clutterbuck, M Devine
PUBLISHER: Basingstoke, MacMillan, 1987

TITLE: Climbing the Ladder: How to be a Woman Manager
AUTHOR: J W MacDonald
PUBLISHER: London, Methuen, 1986

TITLE: Inside Moves: Corporate Smarts for Women on the Way Up
AUTHOR: M Machlowitz
PUBLISHER: Boulder Co, Careertrack, 1984

Appendix

British Institute of Management

BIIM

Management House
Cottingham Road
Corby
Northants NN17 1TT
Telephone 0536 204222
Telegrams Blingram Corby
Facsimile 0536 201651

May 1992

Dear Member

WOMEN IN MANAGEMENT

You may recall that in 1989 BIM conducted a survey of its women members. The aim was to draw up a profile of women managers and to establish their needs and aspirations.

We would now like to take this work further. Many of the physical barriers to the progress of women in management have fallen away. Yet women still represent only 4% of senior managers in Britain. Psychological barriers and the home/work interface can still often act as deterrents to the progress of women managers.

I would like to invite you to take part in this research by spending a few minutes to complete the attached questionnaire. You may like to know that a parallel questionnaire is being sent to a representative sample of male BIM members.

The results of the survey will form the basis of a major research report, which is being sponsored by Bhs plc. This report will enable BIM to provide a significant contribution to the Opportunity 2000 Campaign, which aims to increase the quality and quantity of women's participation in the workforce.

Could you return the completed questionnaire by 29 June to:

Survey Department [Wom]
British Institute of Management
Management House
Cottingham Road
Corby
Northants NN17 1TT

Thank you for taking part.

Yours sincerely

Mrs Trudy Coe
HEAD OF EXTERNAL POLICY

Director General: Roger D Young
Secretary: Fergus Robertson

A Company Limited by Guarantee
Registered Address
3rd Floor, 2 Savoy Court,
Strand, London WC2R 0EZ
Telephone 071 497 0580
Registered in England No. 441975

WOMEN IN MANAGEMENT

ABOUT YOU

1 What is your management function?

Administration/Company Secretary	1
Management Services	2
Finance/Accounting	3
Education/Training	4
Personnel/HR/IR	5
Production/Manufacturing	6
Computing/IT	7
Development/Strategic Affairs	8
Marketing/Sales	9
Purchasing/Contracting	10
Corporate Affairs/Public Relations	11
Management Consultancy	12
General Management **	13
Other (please specify)	14

....

2 What is your managerial level?

Chair/Chief Executive	1
Director/Partner	2
Non-Executive Director	3
Senior Management	4
Middle Management	5
Junior Management	6
Other (please specify)	7

....

3 Do your run your own company?

YES	1
NO	2

** Only tick this box if you have a senior role within your organisation encompassing or integrating multi-functional areas

29

4. Do you work:

Full time (Over 30 hours per week)	1
Part time (Under 30 hours per week)	2
Job Share	3
Flexi-Time	4
Other (please specify)	5

....

4.

5. What is your highest qualification?

'O' Level or vocational equivalent	1
'A' Level or equivalent	2
Post-18 qualification	3
Degree	4
Post Graduate, Masters or above	5
Other (please specify)	6

....

5.

6. Which age group are you in?

Under 24	1
25 - 34	2
35 - 44	3
45 - 54	4
55 - 64	5
Over 65	6

6.

7. Are you:

Married/living with partner	1
Divorced/separated	2
Single (Go to Q.9)	3
Other (please specify)	4

....

7.

8. Is your salary the principal or secondary income in your household?

Principal	1
Secondary	2

8.

9 Do you currently have any caring responsibilities ?

No	1
Children under 2 years	2
Children 2-5 years	3
Children 6-10 years	4
Children 11-16 years	5
Children over 16 years in education	6
Elderly dependent	7
Disabled dependent	8
Other (please specify)	9

9.

10. Have you ever had any caring responsibilities?

No [Go to Q.14]	1
Children	2
Elderly dependent	3
Disabled dependent	4
Other (please specify)	5

....

10.

ABOUT YOUR CAREER AS A MANAGER

11. If you have, or had, a caring responsibility, how do you feel that this has affected your career?

It has adversely affected my career	1
It has benefitted my career	2
It has never affected my career	3
Don't know	4

11.

30

12. What were the main reasons why caring adversely affected your career?

(please tick up to 3 boxes)

- Difficulty in working long hours — 1
- Difficulty in working standard office hours — 2
- Unable to travel — 3
- Need to work locally — 4
- Need to take frequent time off — 5
- Considered potentially unreliable — 6
- Considered not to be a 'career person' — 7
- Other (please specify) — 8

12.

13. What were the main benefits to your career as a result of a caring responsibility?

- Able to adopt a more balanced attitude to work — 1
- Better time management skills — 2
- Acquired new management skills — 3
- Able to re-focus career through training/career break — 4
- Other (please specify) — 5

13.

14. Do you believe that it is possible successfully to combine a career in management and a caring responsibility?

- Yes — 1
- Yes, but only at considerable personal cost — 2
- No, it is not possible — 3
- Don't know — 4

14.

15. Have you ever taken a career break/s?

- Yes, for childcare — 1
- Yes, for eldercare — 2
- Yes, for care of disabled — 3
- Yes, for training — 4
- Other [Please specify] — 5
- No (Go to Q.18) — 6

15.

16. If yes, how long, in total, were you out of the employment market?

- Under 6 months — 1
- 6 months - 1 year — 2
- 1 - 2 years — 3
- 3 - 5 years — 4
- 6 - 10 years — 5
- Over 10 years — 6

16.

17. Upon returning to work, after your career break, at what level did you return:

- Lower — 1
- Same — 2
- Higher — 3

17.

CAREER PROGRESSION AND BARRIERS

18 How do you anticipate that your career will progress now?

- Promotion within current organisation — 1
- Promotion with another organisation — 2
- Sideways — 3
- Demotion — 4
- Set up own business — 5
- Stagnant due to 'Glass Ceiling' ** — 6
- Change career entirely — 7
- Retirement (or equivalent) — 8
- Other (please specify) — 9

18.

** The Glass Ceiling was a phrase coined by the Americans to describe women's apparent inability to move up the ladder in major organsiations beyond the lower/middle grades.

19 **Have you encountered any barriers in your career to date?**

(Please tick as applicable)

Inflexible working patterns	☐	1
Lack of training provision	☐	2
Insufficient education	☐	3
Family commitments	☐	4
Lack of adequate childcare	☐	5
Lack of personal motivation/confidence	☐	6
Lack of career guidance	☐	7
Prejudice of colleagues	☐	8
Social pressure (e.g. from parents, friends)	☐	9
'Mens Club' network	☐	10
Sexual discrimination/harassment	☐	11·
No barriers	☐	12
Other (please specify)	☐	13

19.

20 **Which of these do you view as the single biggest barrier to your career?**

(Please tick one box only)

Inflexible working patterns	☐	1
Lack of training provision	☐	2
Insufficient education	☐	3
Family commitments	☐	4
Lack of adequate childcare	☐	5
Lack of personal motivation/confidence	☐	6
Lack of career guidance	☐	7
Prejudice of colleagues	☐	8
Social pressure	☐	9
'Mens Club' network	☐	10
Sexual discrimination/harassment	☐	11
No barriers	☐	12
Other (please specify)	☐	13

20.

21. **Which of the following have given you positive support in your career:**

(Tick as applicable)

Partner/family	☐	1
Colleagues	☐	2
Male boss	☐	3
Female boss	☐	4
Male role model	☐	5
Female role model	☐	6
Employer	☐	7
Women's network/support group	☐	8
Other (please specify)	☐	9

21.

22. **Which of these has been of most help?**

(Please tick one box only)

Partner/family	☐	1
Colleagues	☐	2
Male boss	☐	3
Female boss	☐	4
Male role model	☐	5
Female role model	☐	6
Employer	☐	7
Women's network/support group	☐	8
Other (please specify)	☐	9

22.

23 **Do you feel that, as a woman manager, you receive adequate respect from:**

	YES	NO	DON'T KNOW	
Female Staff	☐	☐	☐	23.
Male Staff	☐	☐	☐	24.
Female Colleagues	☐	☐	☐	25.
Male Colleagues	☐	☐	☐	26.
Female Superiors	☐	☐	☐	27.
Male Superiors	☐	☐	☐	28.
Others	☐	☐	☐	29.
	1	2	3	

24 **What is the overall attitude to women managers from others within**
a. your own organisation, b. your organisation's field of activity and
c. your management function?

	Very Positive 1	Positive 2	Adequate 3	Negative 4	Very Negative 5	
Organisation	☐	☐	☐	☐	☐	30
Field of Activity	☐	☐	☐	☐	☐	31
Function	☐	☐	☐	☐	☐	32

25. **What is your opinion of the following statements:**

	Strongly Agree 1	Agree 2	Disagree 3	Strongly Disagree 4	
Women managers have positive skills to bring to the workplace	☐	☐	☐	☐	33.
Women managers are no different to men in the workplace	☐	☐	☐	☐	34.
There should be positive discrimination for women managers	☐	☐	☐	☐	35.
Women should not combine a management career and motherhood	☐	☐	☐	☐	36.
All managers should receive equal treatment, irrespective of their family responsibilities	☐	☐	☐	☐	37.
I do find it/would find it difficult to work for a senior woman manager	☐	☐	☐	☐	38.

26. **Do you believe the government should provide any of the following forms of assistance?**

(Please tick as applicable)

Tax relief for all employer funded creches	☐	1
Tax exemption on all employer funded childcare	☐	2
Tax relief for all forms of childcare	☐	3
After school care provision	☐	4
More lenient maternity leave	☐	5
More lenient paternity leave	☐	6
Tax relief for all carers	☐	7
Specific training for women	☐	8
Other (please specify)	☐	9
No assistance	☐	10

39.

YOUR ORGANISATION

27. **Does your organisation offer:**

(Please tick as applicable)

Job sharing	☐	1
Part time work	☐	2
Flexible work *(hours per week/month)*	☐	3
Flexible work *(days per year)*	☐	4
Working mainly from home	☐	5

40.

28. **Does your organisation provide, and do you believe that it should provide:**

	Does Provide	Should Provide	Should Not Provide	
Creche for children on site	☐	☐	☐	1
Creche for children off site	☐	☐	☐	2
Links with local social services	☐	☐	☐	3
Monetary assistance with childcare (e.g. vouchers)	☐	☐	☐	4
Other assistance with childcare	☐	☐	☐	5
After school care provision	☐	☐	☐	6
Assistance for carers	☐	☐	☐	7
Special training for women	☐	☐	☐	8
Quotas for women in management positions	☐	☐	☐	9
No assistance	☐	☐	☐	10

41. 42. 43.

29. **What is the MAIN area of activity of your organisation?**

Manufacturing/Production	☐	1
Leisure	☐	2
Utilities	☐	3
Financial services	☐	4
Retail/Distribution/Transport	☐	5
Public Administration/Government	☐	6
Marketing/Sales/Advertising	☐	7
Construction/Engineering	☐	8
Education/Training	☐	9
Professional/Scientific/Consultancy	☐	10
Other Services	☐	11
Other (Please specify)	☐	12

44.

33

30. How many employees does your organisation have in the UK?

Fewer than 10	☐ 1
10 - 20	☐ 2
21 - 50	☐ 3
51 - 100	☐ 4
101 - 500	☐ 5
501 - 1000	☐ 6
Over 1000	☐ 7

45.

31 Is your organisation:

Public sector	☐ 1
Part of a Group (with HQ located elsewhere)	☐ 2
Partnership/Sole Trader	☐ 3
Public company	☐ 4
Private company	☐ 5
Other (Please specify)	☐ 6

....

46.

Thank you for taking the time to complete this questionnaire.

PLEASE RETURN IT IN THE PRE-PAID ENVELOPE BY 29 JUNE 1992 TO:

Survey Processing (Wom)
British Institute of Management
Management House
Cottingham Road
Corby
Northants NN17 1TT

COMMENTS

We want to include in the report which will result from this survey, comments by individual BIM members. Please use the space below to give your views on any of the issues covered by the survey. If you would like your comments to be attributed, please give your name and address.

[YOUR RESPONSES TO THE QUESTIONNAIRE WILL REMAIN ANONYMOUS]

....
....
....
....
....
....
....

NAME ....

ADDRESS ....
....
....
....

PRESS

The report is likely to attract media coverage. We would like to give the press the names of individual BIM members who are happy to give interviews or supply comments. If you are willing to do this could you give your name and a day-time telephone number?

NAME ....

DAY-TIME TELEPHONE NO. ....

34

Management House
Cottingham Road
Corby
Northants NN17 1TT
Telephone 0536 204222
Telegrams Bimgram Corby
Facsimile 0536 201651

BIM

May 1992

Dear Member

WOMEN IN MANAGEMENT

I am writing to invite you to take part in this major BIM survey.

A previous BIM survey in 1989 aimed to establish a profile of our women members and their needs and aspirations in relation to management. We would now like to take this work forward. A questionnaire is being sent to all women members of BIM. Rather than obtaining their views in isolation, we would like to obtain a more balanced view of the position of women in management.

I am therefore writing to invite you to take part in this research by taking a few minutes to complete the enclosed questionnaire. Could you return this by 29 June to:

Survey Processing [WomM]
British Institute of Management
Management House
Cottingham Road
Corby
Northants NN17 1TT

Yours sincerely

Roger Young
DIRECTOR GENERAL

Director General: Roger D Young
Secretary: Fergus Robertson

A Company Limited by Guarantee
Registered Address:
3rd Floor, 2 Savoy Court,
Strand, London WC2R 0EZ
Telephone 071 497 0580
Registered in England No. 441975.

MANAGEMENT ATTITUDES TO WOMEN IN MANAGEMENT

ABOUT YOU AT WORK

1 What is your management function?

Administration/Company Secretary	1
Management Services	2
Finance/Accounting	3
Education/Training	4
Personnel/HR/IR	5
Production/Manufacturing	6
Computing/IT	7
Development/Strategic Affairs	8
Marketing/Sales	9
Purchasing/Contracting	10
Corporate Affairs/Public Relations	11
Management Consultancy	12
General Management **	13
Other (please specify)	14

2 What is your managerial level?

Chair/Chief Executive	1
Director/Partner	2
Non-Executive Director	3
Senior Management	4
Middle Management	5
Junior Management	6
Other (please specify)	7

3 Do your run your own company?

YES	1
NO	2

** *Only tick this box if you have a senior role within your organisation encompassing or integrating multi-functional areas*

35

4. Do you work:

Full time (Over 30 hours per week)	1
Part time (Under 30 hours per week)	2
Job Share	3
Flexi-Time	4
Other (please specify)	5

4.

5. What is your highest qualification?

'O' Level or vocational equivalent	1
'A' Level or equivalent	2
Post-18 qualification	3
Degree	4
Post Graduate, Masters or above	5
Other (please specify)	6

5.

6. Which age group are you in?

Under 24	1
25 - 34	2
35 - 44	3
45 - 54	4
55 - 64	5
Over 65	6

6.

7. ABOUT YOU AS A MANAGER

How do you anticipate that your career will progress?

Promotion within current organisation	1
Promotion with another organisation	2
Sideways	3
Demotion	4
Set up own business	5
Change career entirely	6
Retirement (or equivalent)	7
Other (please specify)	8

7.

2

8. Do you work with women at management level?

YES	1
NO	2

8.

9. Have you ever worked for a woman manager?

YES	1
NO	2

9.

10. ABOUT YOUR ORGANISATION

What is the MAIN area of activity of your organisation?

Manufacturing/Production	1
Leisure	2
Utilities	3
Financial services	4
Retail/Distribution/Transport	5
Public Administration/Government	6
Marketing/Sales/Advertising	7
Construction/Engineering	8
Education/Training	9
Professional/Scientific/Consultancy	10
Other Services	11
Other (please specify)	12

10.

11. How many employees does your organisation have in the UK?

Fewer than 10	1
11 - 20	2
21 - 50	3
51 - 100	4
101 - 500	5
501 - 1000	6
Over 1000	7

11.

3

36

12 Is your organisation:

Public sector	☐ 1
Part of a Group (with HQ located elsewhere)	☐ 2
Partnership/Sole Trader	☐ 3
Public company	☐ 4
Private company	☐ 5
Other (please specify)	☐ 6

.... 12.

13. Does your organisation offer:

(Please tick as applicable)

Job sharing	☐ 1
Part time work	☐ 2
Flexible work *(hours per week/month)*	☐ 3
Flexible work *(days per year)*	☐ 4
Working mainly from home	☐ 5

13.

14. Does your organisation provide, and do you believe that it should provide:

	Does Provide	Should Provide	Should Not Provide	
Creche for children on site	☐	☐	☐	1
Creche for children off site	☐	☐	☐	2
Links with local social services	☐	☐	☐	3
Monetary assistance with childcare (e.g. vouchers)	☐	☐	☐	4
Other assistance with childcare	☐	☐	☐	5
After school care provision	☐	☐	☐	6
Assistance for carers	☐	☐	☐	7
Special training for women	☐	☐	☐	8
Quotas for women in management positions	☐	☐	☐	9
No assistance	☐	☐	☐	10

14. 15. 16.

15. What is the overall attitude to women managers from others within a. your own organisation, b. your organisation's field of activity and c. your management function ?

	Very Positive	Positive	Adequate	Negative	Very Negative	
	1	2	3	4	5	
Organisation	☐	☐	☐	☐	☐	17
Field of Activity	☐	☐	☐	☐	☐	18
Function	☐	☐	☐	☐	☐	19

16. What is your opinion of the following statements:

	Strongly Agree	Agree	Disagree	Strongly Disagree	
	1	2	3	4	
Women managers have positive skills to bring to the workplace	☐	☐	☐	☐	20.
Women managers are no different to men in the workplace	☐	☐	☐	☐	21.
There should be positive discrimination for women managers	☐	☐	☐	☐	22.
Women should not combine a management career and motherhood	☐	☐	☐	☐	23.
All mangers should receive equal treatment, irrespective of their family responsibilities	☐	☐	☐	☐	24.
I do find it/would find it difficult to work for a senior woman manager	☐	☐	☐	☐	25.

17. Do you believe the government should provide any of the following forms of assistance?

(Please tick as applicable)

Tax relief for all employer funded creches	☐ 1
Tax exemption on all employer funded childcare	☐ 2
Tax relief for all forms of childcare	☐ 3
After school care provision	☐ 4
More lenient maternity leave	☐ 5
More lenient paternity leave	☐ 6
Tax relief for all carers	☐ 7
Specific training for women	☐ 8
Other (please specify)	☐ 9
No assistance	☐ 10

.... 26.

37

YOUR EXTERNAL RESPONSIBILITIES

18. **Are you:**

Married/living with partner □ 1

Divorced/separated □ 2

Single (Go to Q.20) □ 3

Other (please specify) □ 4

.... 27.

19. **Is your salary the principal or secondary income in your household?**

Principal □ 1

Secondary □ 2

.... 28.

20. **Do you currently have any of the following responsibilities?**

Children under 2 years □ 1

Children 2-5 years □ 2

Children 6-10 years □ 3

Children 11-16 years □ 4

Children over 16 years in education □ 5

Elderly dependent □ 6

Disabled dependent □ 7

Other (please specify) □ 8

....

None □ 9

29.

21. **Have you ever had any of the following responsibilities?**

Children □ 1

Elderly dependent □ 2

Disabled dependent □ 3

Other (please specify) □ 4

....

No □ 5

30.

22. **If you have, or had, a caring responsibility, how do you feel that this has affected your career?**

It has adversely affected my career □ 1

It has benefitted my career □ 2

It has never affected my career □ 3

Don't know □ 4

31.

23. **Do you believe that it is possible successfully to combine a career in management and a caring responsibility?**

Yes □ 1

Yes, but only at considerable personal cost □ 2

No, it is not possible □ 3

Don't know □ 4

32.

ANY OTHER COMMENTS

....

....

....

....

....

....

....

....

....

....

....

Thank you taking the time to complete this questionnaire.

PLEASE RETURN IT IN THE PRE-PAID ENVELOPE BY 29 JUNE 1992 TO:

Survey Processing (WomM)
British Institute of Management
Management House
Cottingham Road
Corby
Northants NN17 1TT

38